CW01497063

THE CREATIONAL FORCE 2012

A Virtual Truth of Reality...

Alexandra Oakes

Norfolk, England

BALBOA.
PRESS

A DIVISION OF HAY HOUSE

Balboa Press books may be ordered through booksellers or by contacting:

Balboa Press
A Division of Hay House
1663 Liberty Drive
Bloomington, IN 47403
www.balboapress.com
1-(877) 407-4847

ISBN: 978-1-4525-3831-0 (sc)
ISBN: 978-1-4525-3832-7 (ebk)

Because of the dynamic nature of the Internet, any web addresses or links contained in this book may have changed since publication and may no longer be valid. The views expressed in this work are solely those of the author and do not necessarily reflect the views of the publisher, and the publisher hereby disclaims any responsibility for them.

The author of this book does not dispense medical advice or prescribe the use of any technique as a form of treatment for physical, emotional, or medical problems without the advice of a physician, either directly or indirectly. The intent of the author is only to offer information of a general nature to help you in your quest for emotional and spiritual well-being. In the event you use any of the information in this book for yourself, which is your constitutional right, the author and the publisher assume no responsibility for your actions.

Any people depicted in stock imagery provided by Thinkstock are models, and such images are being used for illustrative purposes only.
Certain stock imagery © Thinkstock.

Printed in the United States of America

Balboa Press rev. date: 9/6/2011

CONTENTS

PREFACE

We are born into the world as pure beings of light, the essence of true love and kindness. To begin, our sense of self is developed during childhood. This is inherited and then built by an outer authority such as our parents, our culture or even that which we see on television or the internet. We develop our sense of being, of others around us and of the world that we live in. As we travel along our path, we are influenced and inspired by friends, teachers, colleagues and our partners. Our beliefs of who we are and of others around us mirror and reinforce this sense of self. But as we develop with these beliefs do we lose the sense of who we really are? The true self that was brought into the world, the spiritual being at our core?

The level of our thoughts may form barriers by judgements, projection and discontentment whilst emotionally we may experience nervousness, tension or boredom. Through this resistance we may deny the acceptance and joy that lie deep within by a habitual resistance of the ego mind, whose patterns lie deep within the unconscious. The resistances we have are based only on our previous experience.

For there is a tendency to cling to that which we know through the illusionary fears that we build of that which may lead us to the unknown. We are scared to let go and move beyond our comfort zones which in turn, will cause a repetition of the same experience which we have created within our minds. Once we exhaust this cycle we may become disillusioned and find we cannot move beyond our rigid train of thoughts and the limitations they place on us. In turn we become the victims of our own minds and are the jail keepers of the thoughts we have.

As Einstein stated:

'The significant problems we have cannot be solved by the same level of thinking with which we created them.'

By gaining awareness of our thinking, we may defuse the energy of our thought process and recognise that the limits which we impede on ourselves are of the constraints built within our own programmed belief system. To once again attune to the true self allows us to become aware of the internal connections made between past events and expectations for the future. These experiences create the meaning and structure of our present experience in the here and now. However, the fundaments and grounding of our beliefs lie purely in the experience of our past. Rather than knowing its own self in the moment of presence, the ego mind, which associates with the sense of time, compulsively thinks in order to be assured of its future existence. For there is the form of thought and the observer of awareness that lies deep within our soul.

We all have choice and the ability to create new options should these rules by which we live no longer serve us. Our restricted sense of self can be set free by the power of awareness and compassion. For without awareness there would be no perception, no thoughts. By finding peace and listening to who you are at the deepest level, you will find the answers that lie within and remember that we are, in fact, all part of something much larger than our physical existence. This may be defined as God, the divine, source or however you wish to interpret this greater force.

About me . . .

Through my own self development and deep faith of spirituality, I managed to break through the distortions of my own mind and find enlightenment breaking free from the illusionary constrictions of 'victimhood' and feelings of 'helplessness' that had developed within my subconscious mind. From this I gained recognition of the profound fear that had been built through this and insight of the beliefs that had been built through the level of my thinking which kept me in this repetitive cycle. This awareness helped me to realise the limitations caused by my ego mind which, in turn, had drawn me to come to the conclusions about who I was.

Having suffered years of both mental and emotional abuse, things got progressively worse and came to a head when I was stalked by my ex-partner following the breakup of our relationship. As a result of this I lost my driving licence, my job and myself as a person. I was totally alone and full of fear. I later came to realise that it was all part of a bigger picture and, in fact, was the turning point for me. I found the strength to look at my responsibility in how my life had turned out and why these experiences always seemed to happen to me, 'a single abused mother'. Although the majority of the responsibility was with those who had been abusive I could not recognise what my role was in all of this? Over a period of time I realised that my responsibility was in accepting the abuse and then allowing it to happen again . . . and again . . . and then again. This was when things changed . . .

If it hadn't been for my dear son, Jack, of who I am so proud, together with the love and support of my true friends, I don't think I would have had the strength to find my true self and combat my fears. As I started to develop my spiritual path I started to look at these experiences through eyes of compassion and forgave those who had treated me so badly. I saw that, as a result of their own experience and beliefs, they were, in fact, acting in the only way they knew how and that their abusive behaviour was, in fact, driven by fear. I forgave them and in doing so, released myself. This was now my past and it was an invigorating experience to be able to identify this and leave it there. Through pure faith and the belief in my ability to change, I broke this cycle, I learnt to love and value myself and discovered just how beautiful life really is. I now live through the eyes of my divine self and by changing the way I see the world, the world has changed.

It is through my work as a medium that I have been able to channel the wisdom of Atonima, an ancient Egyptian scripture, through my pen. I hope that within the words written in this book that you may find enlightenment and the answers to that which you are looking.

Love & Light,

Alexandra

ACKNOWLEDGEMENT

With much love and gratitude to those in spirit who guide and inspire me every day. I give my thanks and appreciation for the inspiration behind the words written with in these pages.

I would like to thank all my dear friends for believing in me. I thank them for their love and support along my journey together with their encouragement in the writing of this book.

A special thank you to my beloved son, Jack, who designed the cover.

As you open your heart and are open to receiving great love,

Always remember who you are,

Your intuition is your inner guidance,

So always honour and respect this,

Your right is sacred and your feelings, precious,

As you travel through your journey,

Remember that love comes from within,

You are your greatest friend.

CHAPTER 1

Enlightenment

"Freedom lies beyond the field of consciousness"
Jiddu Krishnamurti

As we travel through our journey, we forever seek purpose. For we are the children of a greater force, a force that is so profound the mind cannot comprehend.

Through the ego self we try to interpret, try to comprehend how we got here and the secret of life's true meaning. We are all open to our own idea of creation, of all that is, is it what we see through the eye? Or do we place our focus on the divine eye? For it is through the divine eye we open our senses to that which is more powerful than ourselves. We discover a world much bigger, much more powerful of that which we know and can see through the eyes of humanity. When we look through the eyes of this deeper conscious we open to new interpretation, a whole new meaning. We find we then work from a different place, a place where we find intuition, a divine guidance in which we discover greater meaning, a greater and whole new purpose.

As we quieten our mind and put trust in our source, we meet those who guide us, those who protect us and those who help reveal our greater purpose in this world. This profound new sense of being is driven by the force of eternal love, a force so deep within us that we cannot express into words. Through this force we find unconditional love and meaning. A force where we all are as one, we are brothers and sisters. We now no longer are driven by the ego forces of creating identity which fights for our place on the planet. For it is through us that a self that will judge, a self that will work against our fellow humans just for identity, approval and the love of others. We fight for that we seek which the ego interprets as the things it deserves. For when we lack these things, we then dispel the greater force, the unconditional love within us and we work from selflessness self. It is through this selflessness that the mind opens to a more negative interpretation, those such jealousy, victimhood or abuser. For these then give us a new sense of identity.

As we open to this greater force we find intention, guidance and strive towards our own inner peace. For it is from here we experience joy and unconditional love. From this deeper place we may serve the world and help those around us on their journey. Once we begin giving from this inner source, we then start receiving what we give out. As we love from the heart, we activate the neurotransmitters which release endorphins onto our blood stream, the nervous system balances and the body as a whole finds its balance both physically, mentally and emotionally.

We start to discover that our journey is taken with divine intervention. For all that happens, happens with meaning. It directs us in the bigger picture to make us stronger, to help us learn the lessons needed to take us further along our path. For on this journey we discover our sense of self, who we are at a deeper level, our divine self.

As we switch off the ego mind and start to open our inner ear, we hear the messages we receive from the divine, we start to comprehend that which is within this deeper force. We discover those around us are purely a reflection of that which we find within ourselves and may recognise those which we like and those which we choose to conceal within us. For the ego will try to amplify that which it interprets as good for all to see and relate to our sense of identity, for as we want others to see as us. We try to mask that we feel unworthy or that which we feel is negative about ourselves. As we strive to find our purpose, we notoriously are victims of the imprints of the ego mind which has been over developed by man. For it is forever in wonder and analysation. It is sad that the busy mind deters from that which is so simple and lies within the truth of universal love.

Through the eyes of unconditional love we filter these characteristics and see ourselves and those around us through a different eye one that is accepting, allowing and one that sees all of us as one. We start to see the beautiful nature of all those around us and all that lies within our planet. We have a greater appreciation of our natural habitat, the plants and the animal kingdom. For it is through these eyes we discover we are all connected. We are connected through a much larger force, a force of divine energy. It is through this that all is possible, we open to see a whole new world of possibilities we may create all that we desire, everything we wish for is within our power, it just begins with a thought, an idea of that which we would like to acquire along our path. We find that those things take on a different meaning through our new found perspective of life. For now they are assets of ourselves rather than a symbolism of who we are or representation of how worthy or powerful we are. Those things we seek are now those things that will enhance us, things which help us to live life to the full, for our own enjoyment and for the enjoyment of others. For we have all the necessities within us, these are gifts, things which give us joy, things we deserve and that we choose as assets for our lives. They are now an extension of ourselves, an extension of all that is.

For now the greatest asset is our new sense of love and purpose in the world and how we can serve. Within creation we are a source of light, a source which is placed here to find our purpose and meaning in life. As we quieten our mind from our busy material world we find that all becomes revealed to us. For it is simple and not as our ego mind interprets. It is neither a hardship nor suffering. It becomes about the fundamental things we are given at birth but have forgotten. For there is no other that can fulfill us in this way. There is no such powerful force. It is from this place that our earthly life reveals all its beauty. As we look out to life we see beauty around us.

As we restore ourselves, life is restored and we appreciate that which is important. Through divine creation we travel easily through our journey, life has new meaning. A world that becomes far more fulfilling, we are open to that within us which may be fulfilled with simplicity. We find creation lies within us whether it be in the form of writing, art or dance. We find our own individual sense of expression that we give out. That which is not fulfilled by the material or monetary things of this world. We find through our creation that we may manifest all that is needed and all we deserve. A new perspective is born, a whole new outlook to who we are and why we are here.

The journey of peace and enlightenment helps this growth and nurtures the soul, enabling the beings of the light to bathe in its glory. The love of the divine brings peace and integrity to those who listen in the silence to the wisdom of the source. For love and compassion lies deep within the soul and it is through this that divine love is attracted and used to help others. The path of the spiritual realms is one of purity and integrity enlightening the way to a journey of enriched beauty and true inner peace which strives for fulfillment and undivided love. The realms are segregated to the ascended masters and increased spiritual awareness will allow higher access of the divine. As one connects with the spiritual world, each new level brings greater knowledge and understanding to that which is hidden from the material world. Life will then transcend to new meaning. Be lead by your inner source to meet your guides who will then govern your enlightened spirit to that which will help it on its rightful path to the understanding it vibrates. For as you travel to higher and deeper levels along your path, allow your vision to extend through the third eye, the pituitary gland enlarges and allows the golden light to enhance the workings of the hormonal system to secrete and correct misalignment within the physical body. The energies then give a whole new vibration through the etheric body and attract that which may be accessed by the higher realms.

The ascended masters allow their great wisdom to protrude down for acknowledgement of those receptive to this source. For the masters watch and access the highest good through the messages received to the etheric vibration allowing it to travel and be manifest in the physical life. These messages come with divine love and radiate the intention of the universe. The vibration then radiates out to those who enter into the carrier's path to heal and send out the good intent of God.

In the kingdom of man the ancient wisdom of the Greeks developed the ability to build the beautiful Catholic Church. The creational force inspired the foundations of the structure and the entirety of these beautiful buildings. These monumental structures were developed by the skill and beauty of the artistic creator.

The buildings of today are built for purpose of a different source and for the role of modern day man. The cosmetic forces have been lost and the key for the beautiful structure of the monument was lost through the need to build in number rather than the innate structure. It may be acquainted to the modern day man who eats to survive but forgets the source from which his nourishment came and the magnificent properties that it holds to nourish the organs of the physical body. The additives and chemicals are processed by man again to produce in number to satisfy the eternal need to make more money. The beauty creating a dish to use the many natural products to gain the nourishment and water the body requires has now been administered by the needs of modern man. Through the ancient wisdom of the divine we are led back to the natural world that from which we originally came and to find gratitude in the many gifts of the planet.

Through the planetary forces, the speed of light travels to evolve and rotate the sun around the planet earth. The rays of sun give life to all on earth facilitating growth and life to those below. The seedling may begin to grow through the soil and its gentle petals begin to open and breathe in its beam of light. The process of photosynthesis will nurture the plant until it is fully grown. The soul gives the nourishment that is needed, the water supplies the hydration which gives eternal youth.

Should the world be stripped of the egotistical forces of the mind there should surely be peace on earth? For the trickery of the ego mind instills the importance of that which is without, that which is within is the only surety of man. Once in tune with the divine self, man will access the truth and wisdom of the heavenly father. The mastery of meditation has been developed by the ancient Egyptians and the church of the Tao.

As modern day has arrived, the busy mind drifts away from this divine power overbearing the clarity that lies within. The candle illuminated within holds the wisdom of the universe yet the ego dominates to strive and gain that which really only lies within.

As man walks through the structure of time, some are growing awareness, some enlightened by this, now hidden, path that illuminates the truth for mankind. For the solar system has recreated itself to cope with the modern worlds and that which is put into the hemisphere. The planetary vibrations now change to compliment and survive the negative forces of modern society together with the diminishment of the environment. Why does man kill his natural inhabitant? That which was created with divine love and purpose.

Through the experiences we encounter we learn our earthly lessons and some lessons are replicated when not learnt to enforce upon the man who is not wise to his learning. For the man of the ego mind will be shed lessons and they shall keep being enforced should he refuse to learn. Once he has mastered that which he need to learn, then he may go forward on his travel to encounter a new experience. For the ego mind likes repetition, for it feels safe in the light of which it knows. Should it resist moving forward along its path then the illusion of fear is encountered when the ego projects into the future. Whilst it envisages change it will recognise that it will then have to venture into the unknown and contemplate the consequences of moving out of its comfort zone.

Ego lives in past and future as it lives in an eternal thought process and cannot comprehend silence. As one tries to quieten the mind, the ego shall try and pull away from that which it doesn't understand with its constant 'mind chatter'. As the meditative state is persevered, the voice may be quietened and the ego tamed.

The spiritual path is a connective love, whose faith and belief brings all men together as one. There is no trained pattern of thought, for this is through choice. Nothing is separate and all is based on oneness and the connection of universal love. The only thing that will cause the western man to become separate is the ego mind and its forces upon the mind which cause a feeling of isolation. This illusion is created through feelings such as rejection, guilt, depression, anxiety. All of which are lower energies that cause the vibration to fall below that which it already knows as truth. This causes only separation from God. Once realigned, this feeling shall fall away.

The complexity of the life form stalls away from the many virtues that are of fundamental truth. In the incarnation of man, the many values have been lost as he searches for his purpose externally. This truth lives within and through the over development of the ego mind, now absorbed in achievement and attainment, has been forgotten.

CHAPTER 2

Purpose

"In all adversities there is always in its depth a treasure of spiritual blessings secretly hidden"
Swami Chinmayananda

As the ego mind lies dormant, we open up to a new world of possibilities, one which opens us up to a whole new realm. Through this source of light we become complete, we are lead to our ultimate calling. This source of energy leads us to our divine purpose to fulfill that which we desire. We tap into that which we knew, that which we had been taught as a child of God. Our ancestry role lies within our blueprint, for our divine purpose is imprinted within our makeup, our DNA. There may be challenges along the way to strengthen our faith and belief. For some may be hindered and fall away from their path in the needs of the ego through greed, through their need to seek approval, through their need to be loved. The ego then steps in and the negative perspective opens to a lower energy. Those who persevere will gain their strength by the lessons learnt along their way and see clarity to the path on which they are destined.

Visualise a corridor, a path that carries you to your intended and desired place. As you focus towards the end to which you wish to go forth, you will see many doors that lead into other rooms. The doors may stay shut, but others may open. These are opportunities given to you to direct you to your desired place or simply to gain the lessons and experiences needed to take you there.

As we move along our path, our journey may be hindered by the lower energies which sway us away from our intent and test our faith. We may stop listening and follow the mind of the ego. The ego drives us with ambition and the need for it to be feed. We strive for the illusion of idealism. For in this space we always strive to be something which we are not, something illusionary which we see through our human eye, that which we 'should' be. The coin which falls into the pocket of the one of greed is shed on that which the greedy eye directs. The divine child of light sees this purely as a form of exchange or that which may be shared or help another. The matter inspired from this may then shape its form.

For we are all that we are and in the eye of God, our beauty lies within. Through the eye of the divine, we are unconditional love within a physical body. The physical body is our gift that allows us to travel throughout our journey. Should we continue to deter and waiver from our rightful path, we may manifest symptoms and signs of dis-ease within the physical. Should we choose to ignore this continually then the body may wear down and tell us to stop. Through this we are given the time to stop and recreate our journey. For all that isn't seen with the naked eye is of divine energy of our source. Listening to that which lies within will then carry us forward to find greater meaning. The child is innocent, a pure divine channel of energy open to interpretation and its divine source. Once we revisit and awaken this force, we open up to the realms of possibilities of that we may create. Love yourself as you would love another. For you are a leader in your own right.

The genetics that lie within the physical body manifest a certain way of being, a way of being that is inherited through our ancestors. Remember that this energy lies deep within the physical body and is open to re-programming. The ego mind likes what it knows and is repetitive in its actions for it dislikes change. Once we re-channel and place our intention to a higher plain, we may then walk forward and away from the genetic strings which may hold us back. For these may hold you back from your rightly role. Your rightful role is a knowing, a calling that lies deep within and one that only the keeper shall recognise.

The divine light channel will guide you to a higher level of awareness. Never question this with the ego mind. For the ego forms an illusion of that which is not. However, its power is strong and it is what you know. As you open to greater love and understanding, listen to your calling. Set foot on that path and recognise your intent. For it is then we start to manifest and move forward to purpose.

As a child of the light we are sent to fulfill that for which we have been born, this pure divine being that came into this world. The human eye may be deterred by such illusions as image, power or even that of authority. Through these illusions they see identity, one which will seek approval from their fellow beings and companions. The deeper meaning of love will only come from within and once radiated will seek 'like for like', the love of others. For we are not 'accepted', we are all loved unconditionally through the eyes of God. We are not here to prove we are worthy for this is an illusion of the ego mind. Through the eyes of the divine child, he who travels along his rightful path will seek contentment and fulfillment as we travel on to find enlightenment and a larger intelligence than can ever be comprehended by man.

Inspiration coming from within may manifest and co-create our destination. For the connection of the divine will act as a divine channel of energy. Only those who listen shall reap the true unconditional love and self worth with which they were born. The inheritance of God lies deep within the soul, true inspiration from within. The dormant artist is awakened, inspired to lift his pallet. Humanity is given a new higher level of awareness and inspiration. An intelligent mind is given the knowledge it seeks. The golden age of enlightenment lies within the destination of our path. May those who are shadowed by the dark forces of the night, find their way and listen to the light of their inner being.

With divinity in your soul, your source shall lead you forward to discover that for which you were intended. With the eyes of the divine, you shall strive forward to help those in need. For in the light there is healing, a healing through unconditional love. The words inspire and uplift you, the wisdom of God shall help you along your journey. Listen in silence to the direction of your soul, which calls you to your path. For with the eyes of love, the master helps all those on their journey. May wisdom fulfill the intellect and help with the knowledge to the divine light. The mystical world of spirit is powerful for many in its light have the wisdom and experience of those on the earth plane. By connecting with them we may re-connect with our loved ones to gain inspiritation and truth. The manifestation of all things comes from this source. Go forth and master your intuitive cord which will attach you with those who inspire and lead the way to enlightenment. For truth gives greater meaning than a factual world in which those are attached to a materialistic need for fulfillment. For the greed of the ego is never satisfied. It forever craves inspiration and direction, going forth to gain the approval and love of others. In the distant calling, we try to inhibit and distract away from this powerful source that lies within the mind of the creator.

The beauty of the bird song calls to tell you that a new day has arrived. The beautiful voice of the lark calls through the darkness to attract its calling. As it sends its song, this divine creation of God opens its wings and flies high in the sky to reach its calling. For its wings carry it forth, through the air to its destination. As the lark takes off, its knowing that it may open its wings and be taken to that where it wishes is the intent of God. The human is no different for we too need to open our wings to travel to the light of fulfillment. The monetary greed of man instills a knowledge that more brings happiness. This lies within the eye of its deceiver.

For the unknown truth is a greater gift, one which no money can ever buy and one which is forever unfolding through the universe. The loving father shall give to those receptive to this energy to give recognition of truth, to align the soul and be as one once more. The truth of enlightenment opens the path of direction, the one of the spiritual journey of Christ. As you look forth, look for clarity. The eye may attract the vibration it sends out to the source of the creator. With honesty and intent, step along the path to open up to its beautiful calling. Nature will help to realign and connect the soul once again by its feeling of knowing, its feeling of peace. For the seedling that has been placed needs nurturing along the way to grow and rise within its bedding. The rain shall water this growth and nurture its soul. The light encourages it to grow towards it, allowing its shoots to begin to form. The petals of this beautiful seedling form and radiate a beautiful creation of colour and shines into the world. Its beautiful scent is dispelled into the air for others to appreciate.

CHAPTER 3

Energy Centres

*"There is deep wisdom within our very flesh, if we can only come
to our senses and feel it"*
Elizabeth A. Behnke

The colours of the rainbow are a mirage of the beautiful colours that
lie within your etheric field. These molecules of light open and vibrate
as you set your intent and open to the energies that carry you to a
different level. Through these energies, we find a new level of love
and understanding. We find eternal health and a source so strong, we
can regain our spiritual power to manifest that which we desire along
our journey. As you open up to the divine light many gifts evolve of
which are unimaginable with the ego mind. The energy may then,
once mastered, be used for the work of God to help and heal those in
need.

The energies that lie within the colours of the earth radiate and give
vibration, one of which correspond with the energies of the chakras.
The chakras open up to the senses to allow us to be receptive to a larger
force in the universe. Be still and allow this energy to expand and to
flow through you like the ever flowing river.

Chromosomes that lie within are designed to attract those alike, it is
through the power of thought we may then attract that which we want

from our lives. The circulation of energy then comes back from the universal force to deliver that which we desire. Should this be done, though, through other forces, those other than unconditional love, such as greed or revenge, then a negative vibration shall manifest through the lower energy forces.

Set forth of your intended venture and we will lead you in directions that shall be presented to you along the way. Go forth on your journey and always listen with the inner ear, the ear that works for your highest good and the one that works through unconditional love always.

The relationship we have with our fellow humans is purely connective energy. We are drawn to those with the same energy form, inspired by those who hold the vibration of intent. As God works within the divine child of light, he may then help, lead or re-direct those who have fallen off their path. The spiritual path which may be followed is one of invigoration towards the purpose that lies within the soul.

The mind's eye puts out energy which attracts that which is required or desired for the rightful path ahead. Always listen with your inner ear to what guidance is given too you. This will lead you to clear enlightenment, it shall open it for you or give you the key to unlock your knowledge of potential.

Through eternal life force the cells of the body grow and deliver these messages and functions within the polaric system of its force. As the thought matter is developed the radionic wavelength of its power travels to its fellow bodies to function in the physical. The universe amplifies the thought form into the physical realms with the power of its manifestation.

The infinite power of God flows to all those who are open to the radiant light of his eternal love. The father brings many gifts to the beautiful earth plane. The spiritual gifts are given through the eye of the clairvoyant. As the mind stills the receiver may receive the illuminated path of the spiritual master. As the light enters the physical body, the many beautiful colours of the chakras begin to open to receive the divine energy of the light. As light enters into these powerhouses the energy centres begin to activate to open up to the beholder to give their miraculous energy fields within the body. Within human existence these gifts are radiated out to others to serve their highest good. The beautiful colour of gold is radiated from the ascended master to lift and enlighten the child who wishes to serve the divine and help those who have waivered from their path. Silver is given through the light of the angelic realms for healing and divine intervention to those in need of its beautiful rays. A beautiful emerald green activates the chakra of the heart to opening and receiving eternal love and give out into the world. Pink is given to the child who lacks the self-love with which it was filled when it entered the earth plane.

Cosmetic forces of divine love radiate these beautiful colours to the earth child to serve them in the physical. As the mind is quietened through guided thought these energy centres may be activated and gain the growth of the light. The visual colour of energy is attracted to its etheric centre to open and be received by the physical body. The golden eye of the spiritual master gives divine knowledge and truth to the bearer.

As the light radiates to the earth plane, the world is illuminated and protected by the greater forces. The solar plexus are sensitive to the wave of these messages given through the electron field. It is then received through the form of intuition. Be lead by the messages received for they are given to serve your higher self and enable the earth child to live their spiritual life to the full.

We send new vibration to try and enlighten the child of the golden age. This magnificent vibration will help to raise the consciousness to a sixth level one that cannot be comprehended by man. One of which shall take a decade to even access by the eye of those who wish to seek the secret of these angelic forces. The only key is in the divine energy, the creator of its beautiful truth and one whose purpose is to bring a new life to the modern man to bring him back to the truth and enlightenment which lies deep within his soul, that which has been lost and is so greatly needed.

The emotion instills the energy vibration of which is received by the etheric field. These vibrations cause atomic radiation into the physical body causing a reaction which is perceived as a feeling. This gives an indication to the receiver about the energy of that from which it is in receipt. Should the etheric body not be protected psychically and then should a negative energy vibration be received then this force shall be radiated out through its entity and into that of the receiver attracting a 'like for like' vibration. The energy fields that lie around man is known as that of the aura. The revolutionary vibration acts as a protector around the earth child. As this remains strong and vibrant, it protects the physical body.

As the negative vibration is enlarged this energy field shall diminish and holes may be imprinted into its bed. It is through these holes that man may then begin to experience a new vibration caused by the leakage within this protection. When connection to the divine becomes weaker, foreign bodies may start to be attracted in through the energy field and may then build causing problems within the physical body. These may then later build and cause a weakness and the earth child may experience either a physical impediment or may start to weaken within the emotional body, causing a negative emotional experience such as depression. Should he then choose to try to heal this vibration through the intake of medication, the emotional body shall be weakened further. For the answer lies within and may be corrected with all that is good. The impregnation of the negative thought matter tends to try and form some kind of recognition by either denying that which it is experiencing or may form a negative emotion such as guilt, fear or anger.

For the aura is very delicate and for those sensitive to the outer vibrational forces, vibrations of either negative or positive energy could be received. For the cloak of the protection should always be placed around the physical body to protect from the negative outer source of vibration.

The beholder of light is enlightened further by the wisdom and knowledge that he receives. For his deceased loves ones and guides give the answers along his quest for meaning. As the age of enlightenment draws near the vibration now lifts the physical experience and within the process of change, disturbance within the hormonal and endocrine system may be experienced through the magnetic forces being received. As the earth child centres and grounds himself, he protects himself from the results of this vibration. By listening and attuning to his body, he may illuminate that which will affect the body's composition. In the evolution of man, the vibration of the sixth dimension shall bring forth a replica of that which was an experience of spirituality and love that brings humanity back together as one.

The crystalline formation of the planet erodes at the coastline. For it is fragmented by the mineral salts of the sea. The beautiful sand lies on the many beaches of the planet, golden and shimmering in the radiant rays of the sun. Amongst the grains lay the formation of minerals and crystals whose centre hold the ancient wisdom and truth of the land through the atoms of which it is composed. The memory in the cellular body holds the blueprint of the historic times of man. The truth within these crystals also hold many healing properties which vibrate and radiate out through their solid form to resonate with the vibrational force of the human chakras to which it is attracted. For they cleanse and activate these powerhouses at the centre points held within the body. These fragile structures maintain the many vibrational atoms which contain the ancient wisdom and truth locked in its memory. For when these are used through psychometry the truth shall be given to the one who unlocks its knowledge and truth.

The crystalline blue light of divine source energy dispels on the earth plane to man. The seekers of truth that bathe in this powerful light lay destined by the cosmetic forces to follow in the path of eternal truth. These crystalline structures that have been formed in a former time have, now been corroded and shaped with time. Divine energy flows through from source to raise the vibration to a high level of integrity. The angelic forces protect and enlighten those on the earth plane. As mercury moves beyond the earth plane the solar system is shadowed by the metallic atoms of its plane. The age of enlightenment that is ascending sheds a new atomic light through the universe bringing an upgrade of energy to the new age.

The ego mind that predominates the mind of man is administered and programmed by those chosen as the leader. For these leaders of authority possess their earthly power and determine the regulations which restrict and hinder man. The atomic wealth that fills the planet becomes invisible as this negativity spreads across the planet. For we all are one, all of equality, all of divine love and come from the same connective force within the universe. The planetary systems which rotate round the earth give a magnetic force around the solar system. The revolutionary field of polarity magnifies the earth plane. Mans understanding shall waiver in the hope to understand the adjustment here on planet earth.

Moon cycles distinguish the planetary movement and radiate energy throughout the universe. The illumination around its entirety will send a vibration towards earth giving an energy field which may be sensed through the etheric field of those below. Its form is a representation of the masculine and the feminine divine and the cycle in which the moon is phasing the earth. For its light may be seen as a halo around its body.

The feminine characteristics resonate with that of the earth child awakening the emotional body and lifting the vibrational experience. The energy activates the right brain which accesses the creativity and the deep emotion within. The intuition is activated by this hemisphere of the brain and the hormones discrete around the body for the physical functions that activate the living body. The endocrine glands operate in synchronicity with the hormone tract, secreting enzymes into the blood stream at such time when the moon cycle is at full phase. More hormones are then released to correspond with the vibration.

In contrast, the masculine will keep the logical side of the human experience and shall balance the feminine side. The ego mind corresponds very well with this masculine side as they both like to pre-dominate and gain the authority of whom and what the human shall experience.

The celestial light is reflected in the right hemisphere of the cerebrum cortex and will allow the understanding of that which is being received from the spiritual plane. Once the child accepts the message received the vibration is sent out through the cranium base to activate the response and express that which has been received. The endocrine gland of the pineal, known as the third eye, is the master of activation for hormonal secretion. It acts in response to that which has been received to allow the correct response within the physical body through the central nervous system. These messages are sent out via an electric impulse through each cell to finally arrive at the destination where it will be used for a bodily response such as the movement of a limb.

CHAPTER 4

Silence

"To the mind that is still, the whole universe surrenders"
Lao Tzu

Meditation will switch off the ego for then we may be silent and listen to the divine messages which we are given. The inner peace that fulfils us once practiced is indescribable in human terms. Seek the flame of a candle, flickering freely burning with a desire to shed light into a darkened room, for with this light, we are able to see illumination. The stream of light allows us to see all that is within its view.

This profound energy allows us the peace and eternal place which we crave with the ego mind. For the ego is like traffic, running this way and that, racing to get there, getting angry at those who stint our journey or get in the way. The heavy noise of the horns irritates our impatience which feels it's urgency to reach the required destination. We may lose our way and quandar on whether to turn left or right. The ego mind will then try to decipher what would happen if we went left? What would happen if we go right?

So how about using your internal navigator one which tells the inner ear, this is your route and then takes you on a blissful journey along a beautiful, peaceful, natural route. One on which the birds sing, a by-passer greats you with a knowing smile and a journey on which the radiant sun dispels its beautiful rays on your presence. Within you feel a deep sense of knowing and trusting that you shall reach your destination once you arrive. Once you reach this place, you arrive having enjoyed and cherished the journey, having been present and in appreciation of all the beautiful things you saw along the way. You have enjoyed being in that space, content at where you are at. Once the journey is complete and you arrive feeling a sense of bliss, a bliss that the busy ego mind could never comprehend through its need of urgency and sense of self.

Spirit guides us in many ways that the ego mind could never interpret. Through divine silence, the inner contentment that we seek shall be instilled. This silence will open a form of channel that will inspire and direct the given soul. The knowledge and enlightenment given is one of divine love. The chromosomes that we inherit are unique to the individual, distinguishing their true self and the characteristics of the golden child.

Though that which is simple is now confused through the distortion of the ego mind. It is here we waiver and we get exhausted. Through this energy, we are lead to a different destination, one of stagnation and may attract the lower energies of dis-ease within the physical body. Through divine enlightenment, this human shell gains new growth, an internal energy which radiates beauty, clarity in the skin, a vibrant health in the hair, a profound energetic flow in the feeling of health. All that we wish for in the illusion of idealism in the material world. For the illusions created by man are that which is desired through the desire of the ego, that which cannot be created through chemicals nor products. This natural radiance is one that shines from within, one of divine love and pure source.

For as children of light, knowledge must be gained to reach your rightful place in the divine eye. Should we stumble or be lead by the forces of the ego, the lesson may then be re-presented again to reinforce to us which is the rightful route for us. Some may, in a continuation to follow the ego mind, feel the need to conquer its quest or prove the infinite wrong. The journey may take longer and wisdom will then be gained along the path by those lead by this force.

For thought is the creator of the intended. By developing and mastering the mind once again, the ego mind may be tamed and quietened to allow the voice of the eternal master to speak. It is from this force that the holder may find true meaning and may rediscover the true love that lies within. Once accessed this love is then radiated and may be given to others.

The practice of meditation is a tool which will help facilitate these qualities and allow communication with the divine for guidance and spiritual growth through the unforeseen eye of the beholder. The artistic hand is free to create that on paper which is channelled through divine love. Never be stinted by the eye of greed which may waiver you. Always return to the place of enlightenment and return to the centre of your source.

As the mind is quietened, we see the truth once more and can re-align with the mystical powers of spirit. For silence is the answer, allowing the mind to protrude and the power of source to come through. As we listen in the silence, we may hear the voice of nature. We hear the beautiful calling of the birds and the natural habitat which are all part of us. We discover tranquility and discover an inner way of being. Once practiced this may then help to develop perception and new meaning. For all in the world of spirit is divine love and the truth for the higher self may be accessed. We learn that life is for giving of ourselves, we work from a vibration of inner peace and love which grounds us and allows us not to waiver in the power of our emotion. For it is through this alignment we then practice compassion and integrity to all men. We may place an understanding of why and how ego functions in the way it does and gain understanding that each and everyone we meet is indeed a teacher who will help us forward on our journey of enlightenment.

Through the visionary source of illumination, the third eye receives the imagery of divine creation. The wonderful beams of light create a mental picture received by the creator. The synthetic picture shall give messages from those in the world of spirit to allow recognition of the deceased. Particles of light are radiated through the atomic eye and filtered through the third eye to give an interpretation for that which may not be seen through the naked eye. The translation is given through the auditory system of the receiver to give messages received from their source. For it is only through the stillness of the human thought that these messages may be received by the bearer.

The words are given and may be translated via the pineal gland. The words spoken by the divine being of light are given with divine love and truth to help the understanding of all which is not physical and to help those in need of a higher guidance. With a strong determination the ability to hear those in the world of spirit may be achieved. For it is with divine love that messages are given to help those who have lost their way and redirect them on their correct and rightful path. As we strive forward on our journey the truth of enlightenment is given along the way to help the receiver deliver messages to the divine child.

Through the will of God the visionary acuity may be filtered into the illusionary system to give the mental picture of that which is being received. For it is also through this ability that we may create that which we desire. For when the illusion is created it becomes our reality and the ego mind may not distinguish this from that which we interpret as reality. Once accepted through the pineal the impulses are received by the cerebellum. The cerebellum radiates the vibration which will then attract the exact same vibration in order to bring the illusion into the bearer's possession. However, that which is being received shall only serve the bearer's highest good. The magnetic field attracts the atoms of that which is desired by the intention to manifestation through the power of thought and visualisation.

As we focus on this vision, once the mind is quiet and still, the mental imagery should be created and not inhibited by that of the ego mind. The beautiful colours received by the pineal gland are filtered through the third eye and may then resonate with the appropriate chakra to open its centre and radiate the many qualities it holds at its centre. The earth child may be open these centres, again, through visionary sources to help activate the energy centre.

CHAPTER 5

The Universe

"Everything in the universe has a purpose. Indeed, the invisible intelligence that flows through everything in a purposeful fashion is also flowing through you"
Wayne Dyer

Dollar Simpleton was a child of great faith. As he looked into the stars, he saw the cosmos. The cosmos travelled across the starlit sky in all its beauty, its radiant light. This planetary action then led to a new planetary awareness, one discovered by an inspired and wending eye. As you look out into the sky notice the true and natural beauty of these lights that illuminate the planet. The beauty is held within these beams of light held in the sky. The twinkling light may hold secrets beyond its shimmering energy. This pure light energy dispels its vibration through the universe which may radiate on earth. The moon and the stars are within the reach of all men, it is there to take.

The cosmetic force is one of great beauty, a beauty which allures and inspires to be a self that lies within. For the true beauty is held within the shambhala, the realms of the beautiful golden child which lies dormant. Once the child is awakened, it may play once more open to that which it knows and from that which is pure love within the bigger picture of this greater force of the universe. Go forth and play, for love is to be enjoyed and not endured. In contrast, he modern man strives to fulfill his greedy eye and for the acceptance of society and culture.

The greater life of spiritual identity exists within it all and can only be awakened by the key holder. In present moment awareness we may use the power of thought to manifest that which we desire. The atoms of the thought matter vibrate intensely to attract that from the cosmetic forces. Like a magnet it pulls into it that which it attracts. For all is available within the greater force of the universe and all things possible. The potential of the follower will grow unlimitlessly for those who follow this path of great love and truth. The eye of creation lies in the hands of the creator, the fundamental elements of life on earth and within the blueprint of mankind. They are that of true integral love.

The Islamic star that may be outshining the other beams, throws out a magnificent golden light in the night sky. This light descends down onto the earth plane by the ascended masters. Its origin is unknown but it holds an ancient wisdom of truth unearthed within the roman church of the medieval cult. Through centuries this golden light has shone down to hold the earth plane in its divine wisdom. Franklin Roosevelt sought the wisdom of this light as a leader of those on earth. For the research was given to enlighten and help him search for the rightful meaning so to translate and help those who he led. The answers are held within the akashic record file, the files of divine wisdom and knowledge of all the events through the centuries of the planet and those on earth.

The astrologer seeks the secret of the night sky to discover the divine wisdom of this golden light. In the realms of time the divine wisdom of man has ascended and the creational force within manifest the intent and desire of that held within. The ancestry role has dominated through the ages to help develop the ancient history of the brotherhood of man.

Bob Fuller sought the truth of the planetary evolution and sought the mastery of the Golden age. Through his perceptive eye he discovered that other forces lie behind the life of all mankind. The visionary illusion of time was determined by the position of the sun whose bearing gave a destination of the illusion of time to distinguish night and day to man.

The universal light shines from the planet providing eternal life to those in the path of its beautiful rays. The kingdom of truth holds many gifts in its planetary forces. Recreation is manifest to bring all those on earth a second beginning for the egotistical forces have now dominated the truth and purity of the universe and has, in part, led to the destruction of the wonderful life of creation of that which was. The earthly lessons that have been given to help man have been dismissed by the majority so greater forces have been shed on the earth plane. Evolutionary forces have now shown their discouragement behind the enragement of the sea, the fury of the earth in hope that man will awaken to the age of enlightenment once more and allow true love to determine the spiritual life of the universe before it is destroyed.

The heavenly father places his golden light around the planet of earth to produce this shift in consciousness in the hope to save the planet. For the ape originated and sought survival within its natural inhabitant, it reproduced its siblings to recreate its breed. It ran free appreciating its natural environment. As it evolved it recognised the power of the mind and began to change its perception through its visionary filter. Its own development has produced a whole new concept of life one which, today, dominates the mind of man on earth. It is a chosen few which have now evolved within the spiritual realms and come back to the truth of love in its entirety. Though others will dismiss this force and shall live life through the ego mind the eternal life comes through the planes of divine love and truth. The bearer who seeks this gains the wisdom of the angelic realms and the creational masters who shall lead back to their great knowledge through their experience of life on earth.

For as we go forth on our journey through the aging process, we learn of that which is important. The basis of joy and happiness lie in the fundamental truth. For as the ego mind is developed the sense of adventure and need for acceptance within society and culture channel the mind into a process of never ending want. For it is only through the lessons, given through divine love, that our being is strengthened and we are given direction onto our rightful path.

In the history of man, the decades have built an historic revelation of life. The great philosophers have tried to decipher and relinquish the workings of life together with the mind of man. Through their analysis they have developed an understanding of how the human mind works and develops. It is through this that the western culture has determined that life is lead by the ego mind which may be used to determine its existence. It may be used to direct thought into the goal of its desirability through the ambition and wish to succeed within the eye of the beholder. The success of the ego mind lies within materialistic wealth and all that the individual achieves through his determination and direction. This is a fallacy, a false sense of being, one that's only meaning is for materialism and identification amongst their fellow humans.

The eastern cultures follow a more spiritual way of being, one that for decades has been practiced and used in tradition of the spirituality of man to develop a sense of being, a sense of connection with divine love and truth. For this way of life is determined by the inner peace which lies within together with respect and divine love given to others. The simplicity and dedication of the eastern culture preserves all the humanitarian ways of being and appreciates the great beauty of that which lies within, the divine creator. There is a great appreciation and gratitude of the natural habitat of the environment in which they live.

The creation of this culture is sought through the beautiful artistry of colour and fabric representative of individual family tradition and ancient belief. For the beauty of the silk fabric lies in its beautiful embroidery and colour. It is draped to lift the wearer's vibration and to enhance beauty. The femininity is preserved for the women and radiates the sexuality of its gender. The man shall wear more traditional colours, ones of masculine orientation and of weaved fabric. The beautiful colours celebrate the beauty of creation, the beauty of life and the creation of mankind. It is symbolised by the animal kingdom through its yearly calendar which celebrates the birth year of the earth child. It celebrates the beginning of a new year by the traditional dragon draped in many beautiful colours. For the tradition of the dragon sheds back to ancient times in the representation of those ascending to the celestial plane after death. It is now symbolic of the respect and divine memory of love given to the death of the dragon.

The many buildings are painted also in beautiful colour and the structure will determine the family tradition or be symbolic of their beliefs. All that is built is built through their vibrations of thought based on their beliefs of divinity. The many religions on the earth plane try to determine an explanation of the birth of man together with the truth of the universe. Striving to give explanation and faith to its followers. Although this may channel the believer in a specific thought formation and cause a judgment or rejection of those who do not follow the same path.

Through atomic force the earth plane is now reacting to that which man has created. The attraction of 'like for like' has magnetically drawn the destruction of the beauty of the planet and the distinction of many of its beautiful inhabitants. The wealth and beauty of the planet lies within the rural areas untouched by man. Within the earth plane, the polaric attraction of north and south are slowly gravitating towards each other through the weakening of the equator. As we come towards 2012 the land starts to crumble causing a deceasment of its population. For the hemisphere is heated and its temperature is now impeding a reaction.

The seedlings of life now encounter a new era in the hope that life will be awakened to begin to appreciate all that is a basis for eternal truth and enlightenment. The moon cycles are changing and lunar system is now working faster to keep up with the vibrationary forces given out by the earth field.

The astronomer observes through his telescope the many planetary changes that are occurring and has discovered a whole new planet adjacent to that of the planet earth. The retrograde which is occurring in the summer months shall bring this closer to earth forming a shadow across the east. For the solar system shall move and change the equated illusionary time to which man dictated his life.

The ancient wisdom of the Greek orthodox shed a powerful light upon the ancestry monarchy. Their heirloom gave wise words to the people of its kingdom and the ancient history made a significant imprint on the history of mankind.

The radionic light of the celestial forces gave insight and direction of this entire kingdom. In Rome the ancient building was made with the skill and beauty of the creative and was symbolic of the faith of God. The Catholic revolt defended the ancient wisdom and truth of its believers to those who decided to rebel against this belief and defy the laws of the Roman Catholics. The monarchy that reigned held strong principles to rule the land and worked through the eye of the God. The symbolic wealth of which was preserved and monumental within the church of the Roman Catholic.

In the quest for mankind the ancient Egyptians, the monarchy of Montreal was evaded in order to bring truth. Through the spiritual decent of this meaning, man started to recognise the enlightenment of the soul. For the self that lies within the soul was one of divine love and wisdom. The self is a division of many characteristics of the earth child some are inherited by their ancestors, some developed from the shadowing of the enlightened soul and some of which are symbolic of the emotions held within. Each shall arise and will show in response to the external circumstances to that which is experienced. For there may be many different sides to these aspects of the personality type. By acquainting and recognising these traits there may be much to learn of the true character of the earth child.

Some may be enhanced and used for the child's highest good, whilst others may be quietened and used as a tool for learning and personal growth. These many features that lie within the earth child that have been developed by the ego mind reflective of that which has been experienced and that which shall protect the ego self. Our learning of these shall help to administer a greater understanding of the self and the responses which are held within. The shadows of the ego self produce a tool of enlightenment for helping the earth child to develop a more spiritual side of their nature.

This archetypical structure builds the innate character of the being. For the masculine and feminine qualities are the rulers of each of the archetypes. The shadow side of the nature is donated by the negative forces of the character and is often the less dormant of the structure. However this dwells underneath the characteristics and should negativity start to manifest, then this side of the character enlarges and shall come to the forefront. For the archetypes are very much polaric of their different sources and are administered by the yin and yang side of the character's nature.

The shadow sides offer a tool for learning about the negativity that may prevail to allow the earth child to build and enhance all that is good. However the shadow side of his characteristics may influence and trigger the lighter side. With balance of yin and yang, the light will harmonise these sides along with all the systems of the body.

When negativity prevails the child turns away from his divine force and loses his connection to the will of the ego. The external world may act as a mirror to reflect this characteristic to the child. However should the child be ignorant of this lesson, the external may activate the archetype, used repetitively, this character may develop and be recognised as a part of the perceived self. For the ego identifies that which it knows and looks for identification through its illusionary ideas of meaning. It is through this that characteristics such as that of abuse, anger etc may develop. As a result of this others around him may then respond in order to compliment the character shown. This is illustrated through the triangle of Karpman where in response to an abuser, the receiver may then be triggered into the role of the victim in the recognition that he is being abused. In turn this may rotate so that the roles are reversed and a polaric role is once again activated but this time in the opposition's archetype. The yin and yang maintain balance within the character of man allowing harmony to be maintained.

CHAPTER 6

Guidance

"The intellect has little to do on the road to discovery. There comes a leap in consciousness, call it intuition or what you will, and the solution comes to you and you don't know how or why"
Albert Einstein (1879—1955)

The spiritual masters come forth to give truth and knowledge of the higher realms. As we connect and listen to the voice of spirit, we are directed to our intended path, a path of divine truth and one which is lead by unconditional love for the highest good for the receiver.

The vibratory soul which can be heard through the clairaudience of the physical ear brings wisdom to those who listen. Hear the whisper of the breeze through the trees and feel the vibration and peace that this gives within the soul. For this is source, the voice to which you are connected.

The light shines forth to illuminate the way for the lost traveller. Divine wisdom is received by the intuitive self. For signs are received by those aware of the signals to give the validation of the ascended masters. As we strive forth on our journey the pathway is recreated to help all those on the earth plane to give and receive the greatest power of love. Inspiration for the way in which this may be given or received is donated from the spiritual realms. As we reach for truth and integrity, the spiritual laws will then dictate the course for which the leader may follow.

The ego shall try to deter and try to hinder those whose faith waivers, for it has hidden agenda, one of which strives to gain from an outer source. The population may believe that this physical truth is all that exists through the tricks of the ego mind. However, the intention is to simplify and unite all men together once again as one.

Those inspired to work from this place do so from the heart with intention to serve others through the unconditional love that is within. The inner peace they hold is one of divine energy and truth, one of which no man may steal or hinder. For the protection of this inner gift is greatly protected with the love of God. Through this protection, no man may enter through this gate of protective strength unless the holder opens the door. For the physical forces, if persistent, may eventually knock down the divine wall and enter into the physical body should the holder waiver or weaken to the forces of the external negative vibration of those who want their secret. The protection must be kept strong, a delicacy lies within the vibration of the subtle energies and those who hold their truth are sensitive to other forces.

The darker forces do exist may we grow an awareness of them. This energy is radiated out into the material world by those governed by the ego mind and negativity of spirit. They reject this force and within the mind, it does not exist. The ego creates the jealous emotion of those who hold the truth purely because it is that they want and crave but have become ignorant to its existence and the energy of the divine. They will strive to pull others from their path with the intention of gaining that which lacks within their soul.

The keeper may illuminate the way for these lost souls in order to bring them back to the light. However, they need to build an awareness of the intention of those that bear this negative force, for the vibration may eat away at the etheric body and the protection which preserves them.

With the love of divine truth, we may carry on through our journey with inspiration in our hearts and integrity within. The messages received of divine love are given to us through our guides and inspirers. The beauty of existence lies within the beholders eye. The awareness of the present moment defies the ego of its forever deliberating pendulum of revisiting thoughts of future and past. For it is only within the present that we can only live our lives to the full and appreciate the beauty of that which is within the given moment. By stilling the mind, we may focus on the truth and pleasure of that which is before us.

The manifestation of the light and truth of the spiritual realms is received through the third eye accessed through the pituitary gland. These beams of light will permutate through the energy field of the physical body and into the cellular body to take its message to the brain. The cerebellum will then relay the messages to the bearer through the form of thought. The conscious mind may choose to question what it is told, but the forces of the ego are still present within the thought system of the conscious mind.

The power of the creator lies within the divine energy. These atoms of light are drawn to the thought of the mind of the bearer. For it shall be delivered with the intention of unconditional love and gratitude of all things on earth. As we strive forth along our journey, the power of intention accesses the powers universal energy. Once developed the human develops on the spiritual realms and holds the key to higher awareness and spiritual truth. The eye of love shines out to those who may bathe in the glory of that which is received by the holder of truth. They may choose to follow by example as this is the source from which they came, from which they know.

It is said that *'beauty is in the eye of the beholder'*, the inane truth lies within these words. The eternal truth and all that is may be accessed by the will of the holder through the eternal love of God. For we all are children of this divine force and should we choose to open to its vibration, we may access the truth of all love and that which is eternal.

The soul opens and flourishes in this divine light as it recognises its truth and undivided love. It is through this that we may access all life before its present existence. For there are many bodies in which it shall travel, be it in the masculine or in the feminine, be it in a dark or white skin. The soul gains the lessons and experience of all life that lies within the physical bodies in which it has been reborn along its journey.

CHAPTER 7

The Law of Attraction

"All we are is a result of what we have thought"
Buddha

The law of attraction has evolved through the discoveries of Einstein. The molecules that descend on earth are tiny atoms of light which give life to all men. Through the power of thought man may shape his experience in that which he desires. The expansion of the desire expands from matter to form from the vibration radiated out from the celestial body into the universe.

For it is intended that life on earth should be that of joy, pure unconditional love and happiness. Happiness is not a formation that is developed through the ego mind, it is a feeling, the atomic forces of life that lie within the solar plexus. These give off an infusion of that which is felt by the earth child and formed manifestation. Should the thought be of a negative disposition then man will experience this within his reality. The negativity is caused by the contemplation of the ego mind for it forms a perception built on its former experience through the five senses. These senses shall filter what is being received by that which it knows so that the giver receives 'like for like' and encounters a repetitive pattern of human experience throughout their path. Through the process of change, this may be reversed by the knowledge and enlightenment of how these experiences are formed and manifest. By the cleansing of the ego mind and reforming the thought matter, one may change the experience of that which is being received. The ego mind may also form a problematic experience by analysing past and future matter in the contemplation of trying to make the experience fit its perception to that which it knows.

An analogy of this is that if a jigsaw puzzle should you have the wrong piece how shall it fit? Whilst the eye seeks different ways in which the piece may be turned in order to fit it in place, it forgets temporarily that the rightful part may, in fact, lie within another piece, one which is of new experience and one formed of a different shape. The problematic mind, should it refuse to accept the new thought, may then perceivere in trying to fit the experience. These are recognised and responded to with the matching vibration and it is, therefore, manifest in replication. So the experience is enlarged or further experiences of the same kind are manifested.

Should the child then continue to think the same thoughts, over a period of time, they may eventually then manifest within the physical body causing physical experience of the same match. Once more the same process may persist should the child then still perceivere with the same contemplation and ignore the symbolic physicality of the experience, it will become a lot worse and lead to the body forming dis-ease or more severely, to breakdown. For the heavenly father shall try to give signals that the bearer needs to simply change his experience of that which he encounters for his highest good and to realign himself with the divine to get him back onto his rightful path. The everlasting love of God shall give direction should the bearer refuse to listen and be driven by the negativity of the ego mind which may manifest conditions such as sadness, jealousy, guilt or anger. These negative thought matters are then radiated out through the celestial body and may then be received by those near to him.

With the negative thought form, a vibration is sent out attracting the lower vibrational energies. Through the force of these heavier, darker thoughts, the law of gravity pulls the energy of the physical body down. It gravitates to attract matter which will then be experienced within the physical body be it one of emotion or physicality. The positive thought matter ascends to a much higher intensity vibration, attracting the higher realms that resonate with the positive of the vibration of light. It is then enlarged to give an enlightened more positive experience to the receiver.

The golden age seeks new beginnings for those who will receive its wisdom and truth. For enlightenment begins through the third-eye, the sixth sense to those who venture to the unknown truth through trust of divine love and pure faith. For those who question the truth will contemplate the wonders of the universe with the ego mind. For this illusionary perception blinds the eye of the beholder into a false sense of all that is. Through the beauty of enlightenment the truth of eternal life shall be discovered.

As our ideas come to fruition this process is used in the same way. Beginning with the thought form and the universe then supplies the resources to attract the desired outcome to the earth child through its spiritual laws of attraction. As this is discovered new realms of possibilities are opened to the receiver who shall discover a whole new way of being. Through these forces the manifestation is provided. Firstly the intention is put out with the visionary idea of that which is to be reflected. For all that is needed is already here, it just needs the intention and desire of the receiver to allow it to come into their procession. The spiritual laws of success are there to be followed as the guidelines for spiritual growth and truth. These are conditions of the self that are present within those of peace, unconditional love, respect, truth, harmony, devotion and inspiration. They are conditions which need to be practiced to predominate within the self and to dispel negative conditions such as hate, jealousy and guilt which may have been built through the ego mind.

The conquest of man lies in the quietening of the ego mind. The process of manifestation now accelerates as we reach the planetary changes of the universe. The power of thought dictates what is brought to the bearer. However, an analytical mind shall contemplate and produce that which it does not want through the powers of negative thought. In changing the thought vibration the realms of possibilities for manifestation bring that which is desired. For the thought processes which reign the ego mind tend to be for that of self gain in the need to be better and gain acceptance and importance amongst their fellow beings. The eye of enlightenment shall help to distinguish truth, helping to release this fallacy of the human mind so that love may then determine the action of man. For to imagine a life without true love and meaning is surely worthless?

The paradox of the earth child lies within the eye of the beholder. For the meaning of life is within the way in which he conducts his experience. The light within is to be realigned to his divine truth in order to unlock the true potential of his authentic self.

CHAPTER 8

The Angelic Realms

"The guardian angels of life sometimes fly so high as to be beyond our sight, but they are always looking down upon us"
Jean Paul Richter

Through streams of light the angelic forces guide and implant the truth of the light. These silver streams of light shine to those receptive to their energy. The energy field radiates true life, eternal truth and wisdom. The Archangels hold different powers and give healing to those on the earth plane. The eternal compassion of Archangel Raphael gives the healing through the crystal eye of Atlantis. This healing Archangel reigns along the planetary forces of Mercury helping those who heal and care for those on the earth plane. The radiant light of Raphael shines through to give hope and strength to those in need of healing.

The Archangel Michael shines through with the strength of the Gods, his radiant stream of light helps healing of a greater level. Those in deep emotional distress and those who suffer in the physical body. This wise Archangel was discovered in Rome when the angelic forces streamed into the holy church to help those who prayed for the healing power of the universe to help themselves or their loved ones. Archangel Ariel is an earth healer, one of strength and integrity. He brings the peace of the Gods.

The angelic realms which lie within the heavens give help to those who ask for angelic intervention and signals for their presence. Their presence is shown by the white feather or from the gentle breeze felt on the skin. The divine wisdom of the angels is held in their magnificent rays which are shone into the etheric field of the receiver.

The angels of light gather around those below to offer healing and guidance to all on the earth plane. Their divine energy is dispelled out into the etheric field and received via the pineal gland. For their energy is gentle and given through divine love to help those on the journey of enlightenment. These wise angelic forces give their many messages of truth to try to help and encourage those open to receiving and may be called upon to help with their gentle yet powerful vibrations. The Archangel Gabriel shall give great healing and powerful guidance when called upon. This wonderful Archangel who had origins in Atlanta in the wonderful realms of the Church of God. His eternal power gives a very gentle vibration which is stimulated below in order to receive the guidance needed for the earthly intention. The eternal forces of the Archangels transmit their wonderful vibration to help dispel eternal wisdom and truth to all men.

The vibrationary forces which lay the celestial body give a higher frequency of vibration which cannot be created by man alone. The angelic realm work to raise the vibration of the earth child so he can work as a child of God and by directing his divine love and wisdom help to enlighten others. As an open canvas, which has not been directed or questioned by the ego mind, the divine empowerment may be received. The everlasting love of God shall then be spread to help to uplift the vibration of the planet. For through love and acceptance, the relationship of those on the earth plane may transcend to love and compassion to help raise the immortality of those who live there.

The source that lies within is infinite,

Creativity is the source of self expression,

Deep within each and every one of us lies an infinite source,

One to guide and express unconditional love to oneself,

Tap into this source to guide you to your higher purpose,

The beauty of this expression lies within your soul

Allow Divine light to guide you along the way

For love and unity will lead you to integrity.

ABOUT THE AUTHOR

Alexandra Oakes is based in the centre of Norfolk, in the United Kingdom. Alexandra is a Psychic-Medium as well as being a qualified counsellor and neuro-linguistic therapist. Having been involved in a number of abusive relationships, Alexandra's life took a dramatic turn when she developed a higher awareness of the problems and issues she had experienced along her life path.

Through her mediumship, Alexandra has channeled this book from an ancient Egyptian scripture, Autonima, who gives wisdom and knowledge of spiritual awakening together with insight into the vibrational changes for the year 2012.

Website: www.alexandraoakes.co.uk

Lightning Source UK Ltd.
Milton Keynes UK
UKOW050617230911

179144UK00002B/131/P